HAND IN

THE

COOKIE JAR

True Stories, Real Consequences

J. Brooke-Harte

Foundation Press
P.O. Box 333
Port Crane, New York 13833

ISBN- 10: 0692886508
ISBN-13: 978-0692886502

Photo credit: Brigitte Tohm

DEDICATION

To my son, Doc:

You're a special gift. Since childhood, God has given you wisdom and insight beyond your years.

You've been an encourager, when I've been stuck in the mud. You've brought laughter and fun, when I so needed it. You've reminded me of God's faithfulness and goodness in tough times. And everything that you were as a child, you are more so now, as a man.

When I was a little girl, my mother used to say, "You'll never understand how much you love your child, until you have one." She was right. And my love for you, is just a shadow of God's love. Thanks for being you.

Hand in the Cookie Jar

True Stories, Real Consequences

CONTENTS

INTRODUCTION

"Good morning! This is God. I will be handling all of your problems today. I won't be needing your help."

Can you conceive of starting each day with that message?

Most of the time, we live our lives as if we think He needs our help - like He hasn't quite figured out how to make the world work yet! So often, we take matters into our own hands, either to help ourselves, or to help Him. That's when things get *interesting*.

I hope you enjoy the following true stories from my life. Sometimes He has to tell me to take my hand out of the cookie jar.

I'm still in the process of learning to believe Him, to trust Him, and to obey Him. At times, I'm a little slow on the up-take, but I'm gradually catching on. Fortunately, He's an incredibly patient teacher.

When God interjects His perspective into everyday life - funny, humbling, and difficult situations, find meaning.

My prayer for you in your own journey, is that when He calls, "Can you hear me now?" you'll answer, "Yes, Lord."

May you be sustained by His whispers of encouragement, in the midst of your struggles. Be patient with the cocoon. The butterfly's in there.

CHAPTER ONE

THE LIMA BEANS

It was 1950. I was three. My dad was an instructor at a small southern Bible College, so we were poor. In fact, my parents used to say, "We're going to splurge this week and buy bread!"

There was one sure rule at our house. You were going to clean your plate! It was a matter of budget, a matter of valuing everything. It was accepted modus operandi.

At three-years-old, I'd already heard about the starving children in China. And, of course, I was more than willing to send them various selections that occasionally appeared on my plate!

But the rule was firm. You didn't leave the table until your plate was clean! If that meant you were still eating lunch when supper arrived, that was okay.

Since I didn't have the choice of what went on my plate in the first place, the rule seemed severe to my undeveloped taste buds and independent nature.

So it was that one fateful day, the menu included one of my less than favorites…

Lima beans!

Mom gave me a good-sized scoop. I finished everything else on my plate. But there sat my limas! They were staring back at me, like a huge mountain.

Because I was so small, my line of vision barely peeked over the edge of the table. It was a direct line to the mound of beans, which only served to magnify the problem!

I stirred the beans around to see if the pile looked smaller spread out. Then I tried shoving them close together, but that only made the mountain taller. No matter how they were arranged, there were still twenty-three of them!

Everyone else finished dinner and left the table. From the dining room, I could hear my parents talking in the distance. I could hear my big brother listening to *The Lone Ranger* on the radio in his room. And there I sat in what seemed like endless despair, staring at Mount Lima. The situation deteriorated even further because the beans were now cold and dry.

I put two limas on my fork and popped them into my mouth. I gagged! I knew if I took another bite, I was going to throw-up.

Suddenly, I had a vision. An image of the trashcan in the kitchen came to life.

"Oh, that would be too naughty," I thought.

But the longer I sat there, the more vivid and enticing the picture became. What began as a fleeting thought, gradually became a plan.

I quietly slipped from the dining room table, plate in hand, and tip-toed into the kitchen. Yes! There was the trashcan. It was the kind that had a little foot pedal you stepped on that made the lid pop up.

"That will make too much noise," I thought to myself. So I carefully lifted the lid by hand.

Mother always kept a paper bag liner in the trashcan. Another brilliant idea! I would scrape my lima beans in-between the bag and the can.

"Mom will never find them now!" I thought. (Not bad for a three year old, huh?)

Done. Success! Deed complete.

I quietly slipped back into the dining room where I somewhat plaintively called out, "I'm done."

I didn't want to sound too excited. After all, I supposedly had just gagged my way through the whole pile.

Mom came from the back of the house, walked into the dining room, took me by the hand, walked me into the kitchen, popped the lid on the trashcan, and pulled back the paper bag liner, all without breaking pace. And there were my lima beans! How do moms do that?

I was embarrassed! I was ashamed. I was scared!

I was humiliated that I'd been so easily found out, when I thought I was ever so clever.

I was ashamed because I'd been dishonest. I cheated, deceived, and then tried the old cover-up.

I was scared because I had yet another vision of my mom scraping the limas out of the trashcan and still making me eat them!

My only option at this point was to sincerely and tearfully beg for mercy. Fortunately, I was forgiven and received a full pardon.

But suppose my mom *had* scraped the limas out of the trashcan and said, "You've been so naughty. Now, you're going to eat your lima beans and you're going to get a spanking too!"

Then suppose my big brother, overhearing it said, "Mom, I'll eat the cold limas out of the trashcan for her, and I'll take the spanking for her too."

What? Not gonna happen?

∽

But, in essence, that's what my brother Jesus did. He paid the price, took the punishment, ate the lima beans - even the ones hidden in the trashcan. If I ignore His standing in for me though, and insist on gagging through my personal trash, when He's already taken care of it, His sacrifice becomes worthless.

In His love, it's already covered. I just need to acknowledge His offer and accept it. I just have to admit *there is* an issue, and let Him fix it for me. If I don't, I miss out.

❧

Thank you Lord, for forgiving my childishness,
my schemes run amok.
Thank you for the times You make things palatable
which I would otherwise choke on.
Thank You for the times You allow me to
"be excused". And most of all,
Thank You for standing in for me, and taking the
ultimate consequence on my behalf.
Amen.

CHAPTER TWO

THE BIRDS

Grandmom Fielden was a tiny lady. She wore a size four shoe, made jellyrolls, and told wonderful stories.

Granddad Fielden was a gentleman. He was generous and always had a sparkle about him. He was also a tease, often with a practical joke up his sleeve.

The Fieldens were my mother's parents. They called Philadelphia home. And everything was different in the city. The narrow front-to-back layout and the absence of a yard at their row house, was quite a change from the big houses and playground-type yards I was used to. The good thing was, they didn't have to mow a big lawn, and better yet, they had a beautiful city-maintained park right across the street. All in all, they were happy city dwellers. It suited them well, and it was all they had ever known.

At their house, meals were elegant and served in the dining room. They consisted of meat and vegetables as standard fare. I loved roast beef, and baked potatoes were my personal favorites. Baked potatoes however, were not eaten so elegantly in our household.

We scraped the insides out and mashed them flat with a liberal serving of gravy, or butter with salt and pepper, and set the skin aside. Then at the end of the meal, we took the potato skin, put butter and salt in it, folded it in half, and ate it like a little sandwich, usually with butter dripping off our fingers. Yummy!

"Janny, would you like my potato skin?" Granddad asked, slipping it onto my plate before I could even answer.

"But Granddad loves potato skins too!" I thought to myself.

His small gift made a big impression. His act of kindness made me feel special, and so loved.

Anyway, when I was not quite three and my brother, Brooks, was not quite six, their funny bones got the best of them. Brooksie and I were waiting to go outside to play after dinner. Being across the street from the park, there were an unusual number of birds on the front sidewalk.

"Have you seen all the birds out front, right now?" Mom asked, as a set up.

Then Grandmom added, turning towards Brooksie and me with a twinkle in her eye, "You know, if you shake salt on a bird's tail, you can catch him!"

"Really? You can catch birds with salt? Can we try?" I said.

"Sure. Take these shakers and see how many you can catch," Grandmom and Mom encouraged, and handed us a couple of big round aluminum shakers, filled to the brim with salt.

So Brooks and I headed out, right in front of the living room picture window. We ran and chased. We jumped and stooped. We sneaked up upon. But we simply could not get a grain of salt on a bird's tail. I couldn't believe how hard it was!

When I started, I'd been sure I could catch a bird! I finally decided the best approach was to stand still and randomly throw salt in the air, hoping some would land on a tail. Yet always, off they flew. I just couldn't snatch one! And neither could Brooksie.

Tired from trying and out of salt, we went back inside for a new supply.

"More salt, please," we announced with undaunted enthusiasm.

At that, their chuckles turned to roars. And we knew we'd been had!

❧

Recently, I've thought about the Lord telling me to be the salt of the earth. It's made me wonder how good of a shaker I am, and what I'm actually supposed to do with my salt.

What's the purpose of salt? Let's see…

…It enhances. (Gives flavor.)

…It balances excessive sweetness.

…It makes people thirsty.

…It preserves.

…It heals.

…And it melts things like ice.

But if salt is misused…

…It can burn.

…It can make things inedible.

…It can stain.

…It can make things rust and disintegrate.

(Or, it could be scary and annoying if someone is throwing it at you.)

§

Dear Lord…
Help me use the salt You've created me to be
in the right way.
Use me to preserve, to heal, to warm, to give flavor,
and to make others genuinely thirsty
for Your living water.
Forgive me for the times I may have misused
the salt, even unintentionally.
Let me never use salt destructively.
In my zeal, may I never annoy or scare
one of Your little ones, trying to throw salt at them.

Please take me,
Your little salt shaker, Lord, and use me
for Your purpose and Your glory.
Amen.

CHAPTER THREE

THE SNAKES AND THE LIONS

"Daddy, Daddy, Daddy," came my pitiful cry, the volume building a little with each call.

I pulled the covers up to my neck, then over my head. I was hiding from the lion that was in my closet and the snake that was under my bed.

Living in Columbia, South Carolina, at three years old, in a house surrounded by trees and a stream, it wasn't entirely impossible for a snake to have gotten under the bed, however improbable. But a lion in the closet?

Nevertheless, my fear was genuine. Even at three years old, I could reason the likelihood of an actual lion or snake being in my room was slim to none. But that didn't stop the fear. It didn't stop the scary feeling of a looming presence. Besides, I'd already heard Bible stories where *the Devil* was like a roaring lion, or a slithering snake.

So night after night, I called again. "Daddy, Daddy, Daddy."

"What if I call for help and the lion or snake attack before he gets here?" I thought. "Or what if when they hear me yelling, they make an escape before Daddy can catch them, and he doesn't believe me? Or worst of all, what if Daddy gets tired of my calls? What if he just doesn't come? What if he can't hear me? Or what if he has something more important to do?"

All these thoughts swirled in my brain. After all, we hadn't actually caught any invaders... yet.

Still, night after night Daddy came. He walked into my room looking so strong and unafraid. I was amazed at the certainty and authority that surrounded him. His presence alone calmed me.

"Wow! That lion and snake know they're in trouble now!" I thought.

Daddy gently took me by the hand. We looked in the closet and under the bed, behind the drapes and in any other place the intruders could possibly have scurried to hide, or re-hide, upon his entrance.

When I was satisfied that the room was totally searched and free from any wild, scary things, Daddy always prayed with me.

"Dear Lord, Please watch over Your little one this night. Send Your angels to guard her that nothing may scare her, or do her harm. Let her rest in Your watchful care. In Jesus name, Amen.

Then I drifted off to sleep.

ഐ

Unfortunately, children often experience encounters with spiritual darkness. And unfortunately, not everyone has the kind of dad I had, to calm those fears. Since most of us learn to relate to our heavenly Father in the same way we relate to our natural fathers, it's hard for some people to understand the love and protection that's being offered.

I know I was unusually blessed with a father who was a godly example. It made understanding and trusting my heavenly Father so much easier. But regardless of whether my natural father was wonderful or horrific, I still have access to the Best Father, my Dream Dad, my *Real Father*.

And now when I'm afraid, even when my fear is unfounded, or is something I can't resolve on my own, I find myself calling, "Daddy, Daddy, Abba Father."

My heavenly Father, strong, confident, mighty, and with total authority, enters the situation, shines light in the dark places, and exposes the deception. For there is nothing there.

It is impossible for darkness to exist in the presence of light. It is impossible for fear to exist in the presence of love. It is impossible for Satan to stand against the awesome protection of God. It is impossible for anything to come into my life, which is too big, or ferocious, or scary, for my "Father" to handle.

In His presence, I am calmed and comforted. The Good Shepherd has come... And *the lions and snakes* know they're in trouble now.

In His presence, there is safety and peace. I have only to call out and He will show Himself.

For He is already there...

Always and Forever.

CHAPTER FOUR

THE BIKE

Our navy blue Chrysler turned into the narrow concrete driveway that ran under the overhang of the 1920's style bungalow at 125 Ford Ave.

It was the first summer us kids would have a long stay in New Jersey with our grandparents, while our parents were on a music tour. We were getting dropped off.

That summer, I missed my parents and being home. But I did like playing jump-rope and hop-scotch on the bumpy stone sidewalks, while my brother did his best to turn me into a tomboy - a petite, wiry, four-year-old, tomboy. We were best friends.

Grandmom Sanders was more anxious to turn me into a *lady*. She was always a *lady*. I never saw her in a pair of slacks, or any shoes but the old lace up kind with thick heels. She commanded respect.

Discipline and dignity were assumed…well, at least until one of the great water fights broke out. Those usually took place at the dinner table in the formal dining room. The running, chasing, free-for-alls, were often initiated by Great Grandmother Brooks, who lived in the downstairs bedroom.

I laughed and squealed at the antics that seemed totally out of character for these other-wised distinguished ladies.

Grandpop Sanders was kind and generous. There was an inner strength that permeated everything he did. Once a week we counted on him saying, "How would you kids like a dime to go down to Abbott's for ice cream?" He never needed to ask twice!

Grandmom and Grandpop Sanders lived on a quiet dead-end street in Woodbury, New Jersey, where all the kids played together like it was our own personal asphalt playground.

My grandparent's house was old with special smells, creaky stairs, great front and back porches, and an even better "walk-in" attic. It was an attic full of treasures, not the least of which was an antique doll and baby carriage. My favorite though, was the huge old music box that sat on top of the bookcase in the upstairs bedroom, where I often slept.

"What would you think of getting the kids bikes before we leave?" Dad proposed privately to Mom.

"I think they'd love it. But can we afford bikes?"

"Well maybe… I think Uncle Royden's store is having a big sale right now. We might be able to get a great deal. And if the bikes are big enough to last until the kids are driving, it's an investment. I think we can swing it," Dad reassured.

I'll never forget the pride and excitement on Dad's face as he presented our new bikes. I'd never gotten such a wonderful gift before.

So expensive! So unexpected! *So big!*

Since the bikes were a major purchase, we needed not only to grow into them, but also to make them last. *Us kids understood that this was a lifetime investment!*

My seven year old brother already knew how to ride from practicing on some of his friend's bikes. So he took off right away on his royal blue twenty-eight inch Schwinn. Even though it was a little big for him, he managed it.

On the other hand, my bright red twenty-six incher, was considerably more than I could handle. But I was determined to try! Dad ran along-side of me and held on to the back of it, as I learned to keep my balance, pedal, and steer. Eventually, he let go, and I finally didn't fall over and crash. Boy, I was little miss independence now!

The only way I could even get on my bike, was to stand on the front steps, where those extra inches made it possible for me to get my foot on the lowest pedal. Then, I would swing the other leg over the middle bar to the higher pedal. It was like mounting a horse. I couldn't sit on the seat at all without someone else putting me there. And, if I got perched there, my feet dangled at least a foot from the pedals.

In fact, even trying to pedal standing up, my legs were fully extended as the pedals made each revolution. That meant I couldn't back pedal and apply the brakes...Not enough leverage. (And only racing bikes had hand brakes back then.)

So the only way I could stop my bike was to run into something. I aimed for a curb or a tree, whatever was handy, and crashed into it. It worked! Then I hopped off fast, before my bike fell over on me, and turned it in whatever direction I wanted to go next.

I walked it to someone's front steps, climbed back on, and off I went again.

Having to stop the bike every time I wanted to change direction, though, was a real pain! (Literally.)

My eyes were even with the handlebars. I looked just under them, or over them, as the pedals went around. Also if I tried to turn, the whole center of gravity shifted and made the bike tip over, besides putting the handlebars in my ear. It must have been comical to watch!

After my first day of riding, I was black and blue from the neck down. Crashing was taking its toll in my attempts to brake. (Or should I say break?)

"Janny, get your bike and we're going to wrap towels around the front side of it for padding," Mom instructed.

So my parents padded the bike for their determined little girl. I was pretty battered and bruised during those initial days of learning. Before I grew into it, riding was hazardous to my health. But in a few years, I was doing tricks!

❧

Having passed "Biking 101," I experienced a mix of feelings; excitement, gratitude, honor, prosperity, pride, satisfaction, independence, determination, fear, frustration, pain, anxiety, resentment, and poverty. Contradictory emotions in spots, huh? Honor and prosperity, were sitting right next to resentment and poverty.

I felt honored that my parents encouraged me to master such a big new bike. It made me feel prosperous to know my brother and I had the newest, nicest bikes in the neighborhood. Yet I felt resentment too.

Why did I have to be tough and brave? Why did I have to master something that was too big, too hard, too dangerous, too painful for a little girl? Why couldn't I have a nice little pink bike with training wheels?

I knew it was because we had to stretch every dollar. Mom and Dad were trying to make wise money decisions. This bike would last. But would I?

Would others guess that my too big, bright shiny bike was not really a statement of prosperity but of poverty? Should I be proud or embarrassed?

I couldn't help but see my dad's delight as he happily gave a gift that would cause some struggle, but would also build my confidence, my esteem, my independence, and my fun. Lovingly, he held on to me until I got my balance. I can imagine the pride he felt as he let go and I rode off on my own. But he was always there watching, encouraging, instructing, keeping me steady, until he knew I'd mastered the basics. Later, even when I couldn't see him, I knew he was only a holler away.

And then, when I went in for dinner, tired and bruised, salve and protective padding were applied. I was fed and encouraged.

It was my growth on the inside that was more important than my comfort on the outside.

So what was happening on the inside? Well, privately, I was trying to figure out where to slot my own value, even though, I might not have known to call it that at the time. Varying shades of both pride and humiliation were popping up during the learning curve. The real issue, however, was *perspective.*

I got a wonderful gift. I chose to ride it. I could look at the gift, and my attempts to master it, with resentment, wanting what the other girls my age had, or I could look at it happily, with appreciation.

The choice was mine.

My Father in heaven also gives gifts that are sometimes big, sometimes challenging, sometimes humbling, and sometimes scary, but always for my ultimate good and growth.

∾

Thank You Father,
Thank you for the gifts that require training.
They sometimes result in frustration and
unmanageability, and may even contain
some pain along the way...
But these are the gifts that grow into freedom.
These are the things that bring joy, trust,
confidence, and contentment.
And when that day comes that my training is
complete, and the "riding" is natural and fun,
let me humbly remember Your assistance.
Remind me of Who steadied me, comforted me,
and cheered me on -And who always will.
Thank You that You never require me to
do things on my own...But promise that,
"I can do all things through Christ
who strengthens me."
Heavenly Father,
You are always there – only a holler away.

Your gifts are wise and wonderful.
Your protection and care are everlasting.
...Your tests are cocoon spinners.
Thank You for Your love and patience;
For speaking words of instruction and courage;
And for strengthening my wings
in the cocoon of transformation.
Amen.

CHAPTER FIVE

THE MILLPOND

"Look at the snow! Look at the snow!" I yelled, as each tiny patch appeared alongside the road.

We were driving from Montgomery, Alabama to Rockford, Michigan with the thought we might move there.

I was in first grade, my brother was in fifth. This was our first glimpse of snow and we thought it was the most awesome thing to ever fall from the sky.

Neither of us had ever experienced it, falling, or on the ground. With each mile farther north, the white patches grew larger. This was exciting! What were only smatterings, seemed huge and amazing to us.

"So, you kids think you'd like living up north?" Dad asked as we drove.

"Yeah, this is cool," we cheered from the back seat, straining to find bigger deposits of the white stuff.

After a successful weekend of interviews, visits, and preaching, Dad accepted the pastorate at the First Baptist Church of Rockford, Michigan.

"What do you think of the parsonage, Janny?" Mom asked.

I knew *she* liked it. I did too. The parsonage was right next door to the church. It was an older two-story white clapboard house that matched the stained-glass-windowed, traditional, white Baptist church.

In spite of whatever it lacked in privacy, the flow of parishioners coming and going was fun. We understood the twenty-four/seven, on-call availability. It was just part of the job. It demanded family adjustments. But it was also a great perk to have Dad's office right next door.

The old church had lots of nooks and crannies to explore, not to speak of the big field that ran behind the property; complete with a millpond on the far side.

We could walk to school through town by way of the sidewalks, or take the short cut past the millpond. It was a narrow path through the field, where the undergrowth was above our heads. We had to go up the hill, around the pond, through the park, and finally into the schoolyard. It was about a ten minute walk without dawdling. Sometimes it was scary to walk through that field. Sometimes I ran. The path was so narrow and the brush so high, it felt like a thick jungle.

"Davy, Davy Crocket, king of the wild frontier," I sang, one fall day, as I walked around the edge of the millpond. Suddenly, I looked down just as my foot was about to squish the tail of a snake. It was a Blue Racer. I froze mid-stride.

"Maybe I can get away if I turn back the other way," I thought, wheeling on my heel and quietly sneaking off in the opposite direction.

"Whew, that was a close one," I said to myself. I knew Blue Racers would chase you if you bothered them, and they'd probably bite you if you stepped on their tail. I looked back just in time to see it slither into the weeds next to the pond. I waited and watched until I was pretty sure it was gone. Then I dashed past the millpond and into the school yard.

I could imagine all kinds of things lurking in that dense undergrowth! It was definitely more comfortable taking the shortcut during wintertime than the rest of the year. The weeds weren't so thick and high then, and the animals, (especially the snakes) were taking a long winter nap.

As winter approached, the field turned into a frosty fairyland. The millpond froze to the delight of the ice skaters. And for me, the whole walk took on a greater appeal. One afternoon in early December, a few of us kids were taking the short-cut. The main mission was to check out the millpond to see if the last twenty-four hour quick freeze, had frozen it thick enough to skate on. When we got there, it looked frozen solid!

"Yay! No water in sight! It's frozen!" we yelled with excitement. And we all put our feet on the edge of it.

"I dare you to go out on it!" we bantered back and forth.

The two boys I was with, convinced me that since I was the smallest and the lightest, I should be the one to walk out on the ice and do the test. – And I never could resist a dare!

Since I was a little *southern girl,* not too familiar with frozen lakes and ponds, I said, "Okay," and began to walk gently onto the pond. Like I said, *it looked* solid enough.

I was way too far out on the ice to change my mind, when I heard the rumbling, cracking sound, and felt the frozen pond giving way under my feet. A frightening, sickening, cold started covering me. I grabbed the edge of the ice and tried to pull myself out. But it kept breaking! I was freezing. I was scrambling. I was in trouble.

I grabbed the edge of the ice and tried to pull myself out, but it kept breaking. I was freezing, and feeling as close to panic as I ever had. The boys could only stand by helplessly calling instructions.

"Grab the edge of the ice and crawl out," they kept yelling. "Come on, you can make it."

But with each attempt, the ice broke off in front of me. I couldn't believe this was happening! My legs were numb.

Finally, I crawled my way onto the thicker edge of the pond. Hardly able to feel my feet, I started running for home. But the throbbing cold of the uneven ground made me stumble. I felt pitiful.

I was humiliated by my dumb decision. I struggled on, but was so cold that everything seemed a blur. A warm house, a hot bath, and my parent's arms around me were all that was on my mind. It was all that mattered now.

❧

How quickly those, "seemed-like-a-good-idea-at-the-time," sort of situations spring up! It's so easy to fall into them and end up putting faith in something or someone who looks safe, and looks promising, *but isn't*. It's easy to fall for things that seem to hold great possibilities, but in reality, are neither safe nor promising, of anything but disaster.

A dare-devil spirit, ignorance, or arrogance, can slide things in the wrong direction fast, with or without the help of others. And when the ice breaks and the sinking begins, the by-stander's words only freeze the heart. "You must be crazy!" they accuse. Or, "We were just kidding!" they jeer.

They're not feeling the engulfing and numbing icy waters. They're not experiencing the panic setting in from real trouble. They're not fighting feelings of shame and embarrassment.

I'm sure my friends weren't trying to be mean when they egged me on. They were just helpless and scared when things took a bad turn. I was the one who chose to walk out on thin ice, and I alone, would bear the consequences.

Even at the time, I realized that besides making a bad decision, I also misplaced my trust.

Should I have blamed God? After all, He saw what I was doing and didn't stop me. Hey, I was walking by faith! Why did *God* let me sink?

Do you ever hear folks use that kind of reasoning? When people ask the question, "Why do bad things happen to good people?" they're really accusing God. However, the "bad things" that happen, *are the result of people's decisions*, <u>not God's</u>. God is not obligated to rescue us from all the bad choices we make, or that others make, which affect us.

Then there are also those who say, "It doesn't matter what you have faith in, as long as you have faith in something. God knows you're sincere and that's all that counts."

Well, even as a kid, I knew that I could have had faith all day long in the ice and the suggestions of my cheering squad, and I still would have sunk!

It's possible to be sincere and be sincerely wrong!

<u>Truth counts *first*…</u>
<u>*Then* sincerity…</u>

و

Father...

In each decision I make, show me truth.

Keep me centered in You, not myself, not others,

...and definitely not circumstances.

Thank You, that when I face danger,

You're still there.

You're not the accuser. You're my loving Father,

my rescuer, my restorer.

You promise that You plan a future that is good.

Teach me to put my faith only in You,

and Your faithfulness.

Thank You that even when I make a bad choice,

You clean me up, and cover me with Your warm

blanket of love.

Amen.

CHAPTER SIX

THE KIDNAPPING

My brothers and I had to go. No discussion! Whenever the doors opened, we were at church. After all, we were preacher's kids, and that's what the preacher's kids did. Sunday School was mandatory, along with Sunday services, both morning and evening, in addition to Wednesday night prayer meeting, youth meetings, music rehearsals, and other special events.

Dad was the new pastor in a Mayberry-like community while he worked on his doctorate at the University of Michigan.

The parsonage was an easy walk from the church, basically just around the corner. So we didn't need rides to church. It was a long walk to school though, for a ten-year-old little girl. Sometimes, if the weather was especially bad, parents took turns hauling carloads of kids to school. But an afternoon ride home was never part of the deal.

I remember one Sunday my father announced, "This Thursday at 4:30 we'll be starting Jr. Choir practice. So all you kids come out and sing, okay?"

"That's a *must-do* for me," I tucked away in the back of my mind. My older brother was too old, and my younger brother was too young. I was the only one the announcement affected, this time.

But when Thursday arrived, the Sunday announcement had gotten tucked so far back in my mind, that I totally forgot it. I was walking home from school on that cold, dreary day, when my friend's dad, a farmer and a deacon at the church, pulled up alongside of me and called, "Want a lift over to church? You're going to Jr. Choir practice, right?"

"Oh yeah," I replied, thankful for the reminder of where I was supposed to be.

"Well, I just dropped off Martha. She's waiting for you. Climb aboard," he continued.

At first, I hadn't recognized the farm truck, since he always drove the black sedan on Sundays. But it was a welcome surprise on that biting, wet autumn day. So off I went to choir practice, happy to know that my best friend Martha, was already there. And since it was our first rehearsal, it ran a little long... Besides which, I stayed around talking.

Meanwhile, back at the ranch, another scenario was playing out.

When it got to be around 4:30, Mom anticipated my arrival. Since choir practice was a new addition to the routine, she completely forgot about it too. I always came straight home. By 4:45 and with still no sign of me, she started to worry and make phone calls.

"Vera, I was wondering if, by any chance, you saw Janet on her way home from school today?" Mom asked with concern in her voice.

"Well, yes, as a matter of fact, I did see her. About twenty minutes ago, I saw her get into a red pick-up truck, with a sort of rough looking man, probably in his late forties, wearing a red plaid shirt. I was just thinking about calling you."

"Oh, my word! I have to call the police! She never came home," Mom exclaimed, and hung up.

Mother panicked! Who wouldn't?

"This is Mrs. Sanders calling." Pleading, and with tears in her voice she continued, "You have to help me! My ten year old daughter has been kidnapped!"

The police replied, "Just calm down Mrs. Sanders. Do you know where she was last seen and what she was wearing?"

The "calm down" bit pushed her panic button harder, and she blurted out all the details she had access to. As she did, the recounting frightened her even more. Dad was unreachable at the time, somewhere between the university and home, and she was beside herself!

"Mrs. Sanders, I'm putting out an all-points-bulletin. Stay where you are and I'll be at your place shortly," the chief of police tried to console her.

She couldn't make herself stay-put, though. She took off for the high school to get my older brother out of football practice to join the search.

"Coach, Coach, I need your help!" she called, out of breath from her run to the high school fields.

When the coach heard the story, he dismissed practice, and the football players joined the search.

Mom was thorough… friends, family, police, and the football team. She arrived back home seconds before the cops got there. Dad walked in shortly thereafter.

"What's going on?" he asked, as he bolted through the door, alarmed by police cars in the driveway.

The story poured out through tears and they held each other. They didn't want to think about what could be happening to their little girl.

Around 6:00 p.m. their little girl walked across the field and through the front door of the parsonage, totally oblivious to the ever-growing search.

"Janny!" both parents yelled, running toward me. Mom and Dad threw their arms around me and hugged, and hugged.

"Wow!" I thought, "What'd I do?" Noticing the police and the air you could cut with a knife, I definitely had the feeling it wasn't good!

"Where have you been?" Mom continued. "The whole town is looking for you! We were worried sick! Vera Morton said she saw a man take you into his red pick-up truck and drive off. I was sure you were dead by now!"

"Oh, yeah. That was Mr. Nash. He dropped off Martha at choir practice and saw me walking, so he looped back and dropped me off too."

"Choir practice?" Mom questioned.

"Yeah, remember… It's Thursday – First day for Jr. Choir practice. I was at rehearsal."

Incredulously, Mom exclaimed once more, "All this time you've been at choir practice?!"

"Yeah, sorry. I forgot it myself until Mr. Nash stopped and picked me up."

…There was a collective sigh of relief!

… A happy ending to what could have been a tragic story.

༷

"Like Mom and the townspeople, I wonder how many times we're led astray by appearances? How often do we assess a person or situation - merely adding up the facts - dealing with reality - just using common sense - a simple case of logical deduction - only to come up with all the wrong answers?

Some things seem so obvious! It's easy to let emotions take over. It's easy to listen to "the whisperer" planting evil, disturbing thoughts.

❧

Forgive me, Lord, for the times I've bought into Satan's lies. I want to rest in Your goodness, Your truth, Your omnipotence, Your power, and Your love. Even when things appear to be out of control, evil, or fearful, let me look only to You... Not the circumstances, and not the "whisperer".

CHAPTER SEVEN

THE CHAIR

"Life is a 's y m p h o r y!'" he sang at the top of his lungs. Of course, he meant "symphony." But it was so cute that we didn't look forward to the time it would change.

On Sunday mornings, you heard him singing above the whole congregation. His voice didn't exactly blend. The congregation was entertained weekly with his exuberance.

Our little singing brother, Randy, was four. I was twelve. My older brother, Brooks, was fifteen.

Brooks and I were veterans at our "P.K." (Preacher's Kids) position. Randy, was so young and innocent that he approached his calling with unabated enthusiasm. It was contagious. He memorized songs almost instantly, and if he came to a spot where he didn't know the words, he just sang the tune with la, la, la! It was a performance of total abandon at full volume. There was no self-consciousness. He didn't seem to be aware that his volume or style, differed from anyone else's. He was singing the way he did at home... with gusto!

The truth? Randy was simply doing what his father asked. When Dad said, "Let's all join together and sing hymn #402 'This Is My Story, This Is My Song' 'And sing it like you mean it!'" Randy did!

Then the time came for one of Dad's memorable sermon illustrations. He looked down into the congregation and said, "Bub, (his nickname for Randy) come up here and help Dad for a minute, okay?"

The excitement showed on Randy's face. He climbed down from the pew and headed for the platform. How Randy loved his dad! Dad was his hero, his role model, his compadre. And Randy was Dad's shadow. He studied his father's every move.

We noticed that Dad had placed a folding chair on the platform. As Randy reached the stage, he said,

"Okay, Bub. Here's what I want you to do."

Eagerly, Randy listened for his instructions.

"When I count to three, I want you to jump over this chair, okay?"

The look on Randy's face was one of disbelief. In an instant, excitement, shock, fear, desire… everything showed up at once. His little mind was racing! How could the father he loved, the father he trusted so implicitly, ask him to do the impossible? …Plus he was asking him in front of almost every person in the world he knew, not to mention, some he didn't. Even a four year old understands failure, embarrassment and shame.

Innocently, and almost on the verge of tears, Randy looked up at his father and said, "Daddy, you know I can't do that."

The back of the chair *was* several inches taller than he was, besides the breadth that needed to be jumped. The assessment of the four year old was, in fact, accurate. He *was* dealing with *reality*.

Dad responded unconcerned, "Sure you can, Bub. Now, I'm going to count to three… And when I get to three, you jump. Okay?"

A strange combination of confidence and uncertainty registered in the, "Okay, Daddy."

"One, two, three," came the count. When Dad reached "three," Randy jumped. At the same instant, Dad put his strong hands under Randy's arms and lifted him over the chair.

A look of relief and excitement broke across Randy's face, and Dad said, "See, I told you, you could do it."

The smile grew even bigger, as Randy looked lovingly into his father's eyes and said,

"I didn't do it, Daddy.

You did it!"

❧

Heavenly Father – Thank You, Thank You, Thank You. Thanks for the reminder that when I face the impossible, I have only to jump into Your loving arms and trust You to carry me over.

CHAPTER EIGHT

THE GREEN STAMPS

"Are we gonna get a glass, Mommy?" I asked, as we pulled into the ESSO Gas Station.

Have you ever even heard of ESSO Gasoline? Probably not. Have you ever been to a gas station where they give away glasses with each fill up? Probably not. Have you been to a station where they have a guy who actually comes out to fill the tank for you? Maybe not that either.

When I was little though, stations used to give away stuff with each fill up. Sometimes they gave S & H Green Stamps, but I never cared much about those. (I liked the glasses!) Have you ever heard of S & H Green Stamps?

The stamps had trading value, and back then, gas stations and grocery stores were both big into giving them with every purchase. Mother was big into collecting anything free, including the stamps.

Mom drummed it into me to be a good little bargain hunter. It was a particular necessity for our family. Dad, on the other hand, was a philosopher by nature. Mom taught us to shop and Dad taught us to think.

Dad encouraged us to question the "why's" of life. He might ask, "Why do you think kids act the way they do? Why do they follow fads? Why do they have their own slang? Why are some things "in" and others not? Do most of your friends all think the same? Why do you think teenagers want to be "different" and fight the status quo, yet look and act the same as their friends? Where does a person's identity come from, anyway? These are the kinds of questions Dad posed as a natural way of thinking.

It's been interesting to study myself and others making choices, adopting friends, and adjusting environments.

Have you ever noticed that occupations, sports, hobbies, and clubs have their own clicks and their own vocabulary? It's sort of an identification code. Who knows the right words, and who doesn't? Who's in and who's out?

It bothers me when churches fall into this kind of coding system, and spawn clicks with a sort of religious-lingo. It must seem off-putting to some who might like to know God in a deeper way, but can't push past the sub-culture dialogue.

I do my best to be open and try not to speak "Christianese" even though it's a fluent second language. Sometimes though, in trying to explain theological words in plain English, I've discovered terms that previously seemed stuffy, coming to life.

One day, I was working on the word "redemption" when the Lord gave me this great picture.

"Remember the S & H Green Stamps?" He planted the thought in my mind.

"Oh, yeah. I remember the Green Stamps!" I thought. My mother collected them by the piles. Then, she sat down and pasted them all into her S&H Green Stamp books. (And I use the term books, loosely.) Those books were made of the cheapest paper ever! They were thin, flimsy, dog-eared, and held together by one or two staples, which usually fell out by the time the stamps were pasted in.

There was no reading material in them either. They only had page after page of little squares with "Paste 10 S&H Stamps" or "Paste 50 S&H Stamps" written over the squares. And even when all the stamps were stuck in, it still read the same... Only now it was green, with pages falling out, and cockeyed stamps going every which way.

I remember wondering if Mom skipped kindergarten and missed cut and paste class. (The kind of cut and paste that was before computers).

"Anyway, yes!" I answered. "I remember those silly books, Lord."

Then He planted another question in my mind. "Do you remember what your mother did with those books when they were full?"

"Sure! She would take them down to the S&H Green Stamp Redemption Center. Oh, there's that word - Redemption."

"And what happened there?" He continued to prompt.

"Well," I thought, "She took her books to the counter at the Redemption Center and turned them in. Then she went into the store and picked out a lamp or toaster, or whatever she wanted that matched the number of books she had."

Did it make any difference if her books were perfect, falling apart, messy, torn, or with the stamps in upside-down?" He continued.

"No." I answered. "It didn't make any difference. When she turned them in, perfect or not, they were still worthless books. And perfect or ragged, she still got to choose something great in exchange."

Then I realized what an incredible picture was being painted. When I take the crazy "books" of my life to God's Redemption Center, He takes what looks ugly, and without value to me, and turns it into something precious and useful.

The price of the exchange was paid with the original purchase. Jesus stamped each of us with a "paid in full" signature of love at the cross. And now He wants to make the trade; His life for our life.

He paid the price of our redemption, exchanging all He is, for whatever we are. We just need to accept the offer, go to the redemption center desk (the cross) and turn in the books, (our lives). Then watch what He does. We get to trade in our junk for His good stuff. Talk about, "Let's Make A Deal!"

❧

Father, thank You for the fail-safe I'm in because
Your plan creates something good from every
detail of my life.
Even when I make a mess, you redeem it.

So I give You the valueless, simple, sometimes
messed-up, books of my life. I anticipate Your
spectacular and redemptive re-writes.
"Something Beautiful Something Good
All my confusion He understood.
All I had to offer Him was brokenness And strife.
But He's making Something Beautiful of my life."

CHAPTER NINE

THE INVENTIONS

"Hey kids, come help me hook this up," our inventive father called, as he dragged his latest project toward our waterfront, back yard.

We lived on a gorgeous, relatively secluded lake, in Hamilton, Massachusetts. The North Shore of the Boston area, was home for me during my middle years of high school. Interestingly enough, all of the homes around this lake were owned by faculty members from the college where my dad was the Academic Dean. It was great! Living on a lake was a-dream-come-true.

Now Dad's creation of a floating dock was about to get launched.

The first section of a dock was the standard pole-cemented-into-the-lake-bottom, construction. But the second section was designed to float!

"Okay guys, just line it up and hook that latch," Dad instructed.

Two giant pieces of Styrofoam were the sole support of this second section. Now, it was attached to the normal foundation version, and ready to test.

"Well, what do you think?" he asked, as we each took turns stepping on to it.

"It's fun, Dad," we agreed, secretly thinking, "This thing is going to sink if too many people get on at once. And it's so tippy, it's going to dump a lot of unsuspecting people into the lake." And it did! But then that was the fun part of it.

The best part of the floating dock, was the fact you could unhook it and paddle around the lake like a one-man-raft, or a strange flat canoe.

We had another water toy that wasn't an original invention, but we did put it to "other than originally intended use". It was a rubber rescue raft that Dad bought from an Army Surplus store. It was gigantic, round and yellow. It was a bouncy, balloon-type contraption that measured about twenty feet in diameter. Its sides were four feet high, and it was intended for emergency, ocean survival.

Getting into the four foot high, yellow fortress, was attempted only by the most agile, and usually required assistance. This monstrous, floating apparatus had an inflatable bladder that kept the floor from sagging, while creating large air-pockets underneath it. You could actually swim under it and plot tricks in the cave-like hideout, to be carried out on everyone up top. Anyone who ventured below, were likewise targets for scheming and treachery from above.

"Ready… jump!" someone would whisper from up-top, in a benevolent attempt to drown those below. Then, everyone in the raft started running and jumping, thereby removing the air pockets and dunking anyone underneath.

The floating dock and the rubber rescue raft were not the end of dad's water toys, either. He never ran out of fun ideas. His next project required more huge pieces of Styrofoam. It was his "piece de resistance"…the paddle-wheel bike.

My wonderful bike, that special gift from when I was four, had weathered several personally customized paint jobs, various parade decorations, and riding service beyond the call of duty. It had been a faithful servant for many years. It had, in fact, lasted until I was driving, as a lifetime investment. At sixteen, it was now time for its new role. "Are you willing to give up your bike, Jan? Can I use it to make a paddlewheel bike?" Dad asked.

Since the car had basically replaced the bike by now, I agreed, and Dad began to create.

First, he built a big wooden paddlewheel. Then he took my old bike and attached it to two, six foot-by-two foot sections of Styrofoam. He hooked two normal bike chains together and ran them from the bike sprocket to the paddlewheel sprocket. Voila - Paddlewheel Bike!

If you balanced carefully on the Styrofoam pontoons, you could climb aboard the bike and get out on to the lake. The problem was that its size and weight made for a really bulky, slow-moving, vehicle. And if there was a strong wind, your best efforts were no match! Peddling as hard as you could, you still went backwards. The wind always won. On breezy days, you were simply destined to sail backwards across the lake in reverse.

But that wasn't the worst part of it. As you peddled, the chain would inevitably stretch, loosen, and fall off. The only option was to get off the bike, try to balance on the Styrofoam pontoons, and put the chain back on. Of course, while you did this, you also drifted. The wind definitely moved the vehicle faster than the paddlewheel did! Any who attempted to captain this ship, began to identify with those lost at sea for days... weeks... months.

"Forget it! I'm jumping in and pushing this thing back to shore!" I mumbled to myself, admitting defeat, after the fifth time the chain came off.

I have to say, though, in spite of the glitches, we had fun! We laughed over the pranks, and all of Dad's inventions. And we loved living on the lake, which inspired them.

But then there was the night that the bad storm hit. Lightening flashed and the wind raged. At the crack of dawn, we went out to assess the damages, and discovered that the rubber raft and the paddlewheel-bike were gone... Vanished!

I disconnected the section of floating dock and began to paddle around the lake in search of the missing pair.

"I found them!" I announced, as I beached my flat canoe. "They sailed away on their own, and they're hiding in a little alcove at the other end of the lake, like a couple of prodigals."

Now, the problem was how to gather the wanderers and return them to port. This was going to be a tough one. It was definitely more than a one man job. A couple of helpers, a couple of hours, and a lot of work later, it was "mission accomplished".

This time we doubly anchored them. We could only wait to see if our efforts would pay off in the next storm. We didn't want to lose them again. We would do whatever it took to keep them secure, or if necessary, to bring them home again.

ॐ

I can identify with Dad's inventions. There are times when I have probably been a little like the Styrofoam dock... versatile and fun... But walk softly, or you might carry a wet stick.

I'm a little like the rubber life-raft, too. I'm safe unless punctured, and of course, useful for tricks, schemes, and laughs. Also, available for recreation or rescue. But am I seaworthy? And might it be too risky, or too much effort for others to climb over my walls and get inside my heart?

And then there's the paddlewheel boat. I can definitely identify with that one. I've often peddled against the wind, maintaining a standstill, or running backwards... my chain coming off, setting me adrift, then scrambling, trying to repair it to get back on course, only to have a repeat scenario. How many times have I been, figuratively, stranded in the middle of the lake?

Yet always, somehow, I'm carried safely back to shore.

And then, of course, there are the times I've taken my own course in the storm. I've run my own prodigal race to the hiding place... My own little alcove. Or there are times, I've quietly slipped loose, become un-tethered, and been blown to distant shores.

ೖ

Lord, thank You for always coming to find me.
Thank You for seeking after me and not giving up.
Thank You for sending out the rescue squad to
bring me safely home.
And thank You for not ridiculing or condemning me,
but rather, gently and securely tethering
the anchor once again.

CHAPTER TEN

THE CHOICE

"The car just quit. ...Praise the Lord!" "The basement flooded again. ...Praise the Lord!"

Back in the 1970's, the phrase "Praise the Lord" got used almost like Christian slang. At that time, during the days of the *Jesus Movement,* a new awareness took hold of our need to give thanks... That was good! On the other hand, at times it seemed insincere and just something "good Christians" were supposed to say.

Actually, no matter what the era, insincere words may roll out like rehearsed, meaningless, spiritual responses... And that's not good.

But sincerely, what is the biblical instruction "In everything give thanks, Rejoice always," all about?

Why have we been told to do something so contrary to our natural and honest inclinations?

Personally, I've struggled with it. For me, giving thanks for stuff that's "not good" strikes me as insincere. I mean, how can you give thanks for things that are devastating or rotten? Wouldn't that be bogus… even wrong?

In my mind, there could only be two choices. Either giving thanks in all things was phony, or it was attributing bad to God. Neither were acceptable to me.

On the other hand, I couldn't deny there was truth, even comfort, in the concept of living in a consistent attitude of thanksgiving.

Is it possible that it actually works? *How can it be possible* in a practical way?

One day, I was visiting with a friend and we started talking about it. I expressed my frustration. "I just don't get how this all fits together," I complained. He came up with a story-picture I thought was great.

He said, "Suppose you went out and bought a new bike for your son, and when you gave it to him he said, 'Gee thanks, Mom. This is great! I love it.'

Well, that would be good, *and* as it should be, right?"

"Right," I agreed.

Well, suppose another time, he came to you wanting to go somewhere with a bunch of his friends, and you told him "No," and he went away angry. But then suppose a little while later, he came back and said, "Sorry I got mad, Mom. Thanks for not letting me go. I don't understand. But I trust you. You have a better plan, right?"

"Wow!" I said. "That would be real love. That would be real trust."

৯

So how does that apply to *me* having a thankful heart?

I guess the question is simply, "Do I trust Him?" Do I believe Him when He says, "In everything give thanks. Rejoice always!" Am I willing to bypass my feelings and obey, even if what I consider tragedy or disappointment strikes?

Do I really believe that He loves me and is working all things for my good?

I know the answer to that question makes all the difference in how I live my life.

❧

Dear Lord, I so often just trust myself.
I sometimes find that regardless of my words,
I'm living life as if You don't exist.
I'm amazed at my resistance to truth when it
reaches out of my comfort zone or
doesn't make sense to me.
I'm disconcerted by my lack of discipline
to choose to give thanks and rejoice.
Please forgive my arrogant willfulness
and lack of trust.
I know that You only give me this instruction
because it's the key to happiness and to my love
relationship with You.
I'm choosing now, to thank You, to praise You, and
to trust You. King of Kings, Lord of Lords,
Prince of Peace, Wonderful Counselor, Mighty
God, Everlasting Father… You are glorious and
worthy of praise. Amen.

CHAPTER ELEVEN

THE NICKLE AND THE SILVER DOLLAR

Does any boy or girl have a dime with him today?" Dad asked, beginning his object lesson. He was filling in as the guest minister at a local church.

He was teaching about the exchange principle found in scripture. He was explaining our options.

"We can exchange our loneliness for the Lord's companionship. He promises that He 'will never leave us or forsake us.'

We can exchange our fear for His love. 'Perfect love casts out fear.'

We can exchange our failures for His forgiveness.

'If we confess our sins, He is faithful and just to forgive us our sins and to cleanse us from all unrighteousness.'"

He emphasized, *"Whenever we accept the offer, we get to make the trade."* When he got no response with the dime question, he tried again.

"Okay, does anyone have a nickel?"

Sitting in the back row, I was waiting for his recovery, and realized he was experiencing a very shy, or a very dry group. I wanted to see how he was going to navigate this one.

Eventually, a little boy about four years old held up his hand and said, "I have a nickel."

Dad called him up to the platform. As he climbed the stairs, Dad pulled a silver dollar from his pocket.

"What's your name?" he asked.

A bashful, "Timmy," was the response.

"Well, Timmy, how old are you?"

Four little fingers shot into the air.

"Do you know what this is I'm holding in my hand?"

Timmy stared at the large coin, but said nothing.

"It's a silver dollar, Tim. And I'll tell you what I'm going to do. I'll trade you this bright, shiny silver dollar for your nickel, okay?"

Timmy quietly studied the silver dollar. But his fist remained tightly clenched around the nickel. He shook his head, "No."

A slight sympathetic tension rippled through the congregation.

"Maybe you don't understand," Dad continued, "This silver dollar is worth lots and lots of nickels. What do you say? You give me your nickel and I'll give you my silver dollar. No strings attached, okay?"

Once again, Tim thought for a few seconds. Then he solemnly shook his head no, again.

No matter what Dad tried, he never could get him to trade his nickel for the silver dollar. At first it seemed like one sermon illustration was down-the-drain. But then the lights came on.

God knew the real illustration.

Most of us refuse the trade!

ॐ

Sometimes I hold on to failures, fear, and loneliness... *my nickels*, because I'm comfortable with them. I've earned them. I understand them. They belong to me. I own them.

And when God comes to me offering an incredible exchange, no strings attached, I shake my head, "No". Motivated by mistrust, caution, or just ownership, I reject God's gift and cling to my ridiculous poverty, while usually complaining about it, to boot.

I wonder, why is it so hard to lay down the nickels? Physical, emotional, and spiritual prosperity depend on it. God will not pry open my fingers. I have to let go. I have to learn to trust.

❧

I want to lift open hands to You, Lord, in worship and praise. I acknowledge I can't receive Your silver dollars with clenched fists.
Thank you for Your patience, as I let go of my nickels and receive Your wonderful exchange.
Amen.

CHAPTER TWELVE

THE COOKIE CAPER

It was a long narrow kitchen with lots of metal cabinets and drawers. It was sort of a toddler-explorer's paradise, opening and closing troughs of delightful treasures.

The best and most important drawer, however, was the one with the Salerno Butter Cookies in it.

Some days my little son, Brad, thought nothing was more fun than to pull cans out of the cabinets and stack them like blocks. Dishes, cups and saucers, pots, lids, and utensils, were easily transformed into drums or building materials. They were easy to get at too, in this kitchen where all the drawers and cabinet doors opened easily, and child-proof latches had yet to be invented.

Brad's favorite address was Sesame Street, and the Cookie Monster was an important friend. He used to say "C o o k i e" just like Cookie Monster did. It always made me laugh. And then he got to go into the special drawer and get a cookie. We had an agreement that cookies were okay as long as he remembered the rule, "One cookie at a time and not too many times a day."

Then one day it happened! I rounded the corner and glanced into the kitchen. Quickly, I dodged back out of sight and tried to stifle a laugh, as I literally shook.

There, sitting on the floor with his back against the cupboards, was my *little angel*. He was completely surrounded by Salerno Butter Cookies. They spread across the floor and between his legs. His fists bulged with cookies. His little cheeks ballooned, as he chewed and stuffed.

Raisin, his miniature French Poodle side-kick, was in on it too. Both of them were eating as fast as they could, completely unaware they'd been found out.

Butter cookies were his favorite! All I could figure was that instead of reaching into the cookie drawer and getting one cookie, he must have pulled out the whole new box. Then trying to open it while it teetered on the edge of the drawer, undoubtedly, it crashed and scattered cookies everywhere.

I saw his little wheels turning. "All of these cookies! And just me and Raisin to destroy the evidence!"

The scene was so funny, my natural reaction was to laugh! But on the other hand, I remembered my dad's advice about consistency. Laughing at something when they're little because it's cute, may not be so cute when they're big and the innocence is gone.

With this admonition in mind, I ducked back around the corner to regain my composure and think it through, before facing the unfolding cookie caper. When I finally stopped laughing, I walked into the kitchen and calmly said, "Brad, what happened?" My tone was matter-of-fact... but to no avail.

When I asked what I thought was a non-threatening question, Brad's little eyes filled with tears. He spit the cookies out of his mouth, dropped the cookies from his clenched hands, and began crying and running at the same time.

Now *I was* the sad one. Immediately, I caught him and scooped him up in my arms.

"It's okay honey, I began. Next time you want a cookie, just reach in and get one. Don't try to pull-out the whole box. They can spill, huh? Did you think if you ate them all before I came in, I wouldn't know what happened? It's all right. I know it was an accident.

You can always come and tell Mom. Mommy loves you so much. You know I don't care if you have cookies. But if you ate the whole box, they might make you sick. Then you might not even like them anymore."

The problem was the "ol' cover up" at work again.

…Memories of lima beans for me. Same song, different verse. Mine didn't begin as an accident, though.

The situation was so cute I didn't *want* to address it at all! Questions raced through my head. But would that send the wrong message? Would it reinforce the cover-up? Could it suggest that deception, (which usually ends up as a plain old lie) doesn't matter? What if by ignoring it, the principles of trying to hide mistakes and not owning-up, become a not-so-funny habit later in life?

I hated that I made my son cry over something so cute. I mean, he cleaned up the mess and wasn't wasteful, all at the same time. He and Raisin almost got away with it too!

If luck had been on their side, they could have eaten a whole box of cookies they loved, and might have not have had to admit to either the accident or the cover-up. Yep. They almost pulled it off.

☙

I wonder how many times the Lord wishes it wasn't necessary to confront me with some of my rationalized, two-year-old type decisions? I've said so many times, "Gee, I can't get away with anything. It seems like I always get caught no matter what! *If, the Lord chastens those He loves, He must love me a lot!*

I know He's trying to get my hand out of the cookie jar, before I get sick. He feeds me the "bread of life," calls me to a balanced diet, and curbs the junk food. I don't think He wants to spoil my fun; He just doesn't want me sick or damaged.

☙

Thank You, Lord, for flagging my plays, when I cross the line of our agreement, or enter into off-limits territory. I know it's for my own good.
I want to learn Your ways.
Thank You for all the cookies You let me have.
And thank You for Your gentle confrontation and correction when accidental or intentional opportunities arise,

that would allow me to rationalize compromises,
or pursue situational ethics,
that result in unwise choices.
I don't want to depend on my own wisdom or
cleverness to gain needs, or treats.
You know my favorite cookies, and how many I can
handle without them threatening me spiritually,
emotionally or physically.
Thank You for Your generosity, Lord.
Thanks for forgiving me when
I make foolish choices.
Thank You that Your sight is clear
and Your perspective is accurate.
Your love, and divine influence on my heart,
and its reflection in my life,
are the overriding blessings of my existence.
Thanks for a sense of humor too. Teach me to
treasure all of the funny things You bring to me
every day. I want to laugh more, Lord,
even in the midst of lessons.
I'd much rather learn laughing, than crying.
Help me not to take myself so seriously.

I don't want tears to be the only way

You can get my attention.

You created laughter...

You created cookies.

You created a time for both. Thanks.

HAND IN THE COOKIE JAR

CHAPTER THIRTEEN
THE SPEAKING ENGAGEMENT

"Time to get up!" she announced in her own inimitable way. I felt a leap onto the end of the bed. Our miniature poodle was starting off the day with her *good-morning* bound.

Before being fully awake, I realized she ate the plants again, and the inevitable result was being deposited as she heaved pitifully all over the covers.

I jumped out of bed and began to clean up the mess which had soaked through the bedspread, blanket and sheets. Everything had to be washed.

"Hmm… This isn't exactly the way I wanted to start the day," I thought, as I threw in the first load of wash, and got breakfast ready. I could hear my four year old playing in his room. It was time to get him up and ready for the day too, along with helping my husband off to work. Everything was in high gear.

This little twist-de-jour wasn't any big deal. After all, "Handle it, handle it, handle it!" was my motto.

However, as the day wore on, it turned out to be only the forerunner of a day full of interruptions and emergencies. They came non-stop. Normally, I take surprises and unusual events in stride. But this day was different. This day I was scheduled to speak to the women of one of the first mega churches in the area, on the subject of, *The Place of Women in Today's Society*. These were sophisticated women whose husbands, for the most part, were big business men, doctors and lawyers.

I was only twenty-six. I'd been to some great seminars on the subject. So, I felt like I had a pretty good handle on the balance between being a godly woman and being a women's libber. But the challenge and slight absurdity of it all was starting to hit me, even though, it was an honor to be invited.

The day before, I made some notes…fourteen pages worth to be exact. "Wow, this isn't a half hour speech, this is week-end seminar!" I thought.

"Oh well, I'll cut it down to size tomorrow. I'll have plenty of time to refine it later," I convinced myself.

But now, my tomorrow had been confiscated. I kept thinking, "I have to get to those notes!" No matter how hard I tried though, something interrupted and commandeered my attention. When 4:00 p.m. arrived, I was in the family room foolishly folding wash, as I tried to remember what on earth I'd written the day before. There were now tears flowing down my face.

I still had to get cleaned up, clothes changed, dinner made, notes edited, and drive to the church to speak. The meeting was at seven. I was down to three hours and counting.

Sesame Street was playing in the background and my little son was glued to it. Then he looked over and saw the tears streaming down my face.

"What's wrong, Mommy?" he asked with such sincere concern that it took me off guard.

"Well, I have to speak to the women at the church tonight and I'm not prepared. I guess I'm scared," I confessed to the innocent, listening ears.

His eyes grew wide, as he looked at me in shock and said, "You're scared?" There was total disbelief in his voice that his mother could be scared.

"Yeah, I'm scared," I admitted.

He continued with a question that was disarming. "Don't you know Who's always with you? Let's pray right now," he said, and bowed his little head.

"Dear Jesus, please help Mommy to remember that You're always with her. Amen."

That was it; simple and to the point. It was so what I needed to remember. So what I needed to hear. Now the tears were really running down my face!

"Thanks honey. You're right. Jesus is always with us. Thanks for praying for me. I needed that," I said.

ᔐ

I have no idea what I said to those ladies that night. It went fine, but it was likely not earth shaking to the more seasoned listeners.

What shook my world, though, is what my son said to me. "Don't you know Who's always with you, Mommy?" That's the best thing ever! I'll never forget it.

No matter what place we hold in society, what the task, or where the assignment…Jesus is always there. He goes before and He comes after.

ᔐ

Thank you, Lord, for the lessons we learn out of the mouths of babes. Thank You that You've promised You will never leave us or forsake us.
Thank You for reminding us that if You are for us, who can be against us?
Thank You for carrying us over rough spots and covering our words with Your grace.
May the world see only You, in us.
Amen.

CHAPTER FOURTEEN

THE TICKET

As usual, I was trying to cram too many things into too little time. It was my son's eighth birthday. I was in a huge rush to get home and get the party ready. In my race, I accelerated when I hit the straight stretch of road parallel to the highway.

The speed limit was residential, since houses ran along one side of the street. But I could see that I had a clear shot. -Not another car on the road. Yes, it was just me... and the police officer who was sitting in the parking area behind the big gray house. He pulled out with lights flashing and sirens blaring. Then he ticketed me for doing sixty-five in a thirty-five.

I was devastated. The ticket was going to cost me $85.00! (And that was a lot of money back in 1977.) My only possible recourse was to go down to the courthouse and plead my case. Hopefully, the fine could at least be reduced. I didn't have the money to pay for it, no matter how much I deserved it. So on a whim, I went down to the courthouse prior to the actual court date.

"The judge is in session. If you want to wait a couple of minutes, I can arrange for the case to be heard right now, and that will save you another trip down here," one of the officials kindly informed me.

"Uh Oh!" ran through my mind. I only intended to ask a few questions and check out my options. I didn't plan on pleading my case before the judge. That wasn't what I had in mind.

"Oh thanks," I responded. Internally though, I was gulping! "Yeah, I guess I might as well get it over with since I'm down here," I finally conceded. The die was cast.

I walked into the back of the courtroom. It was totally empty except for the judge, the bailiff, and two clerks, whose office windows opened up to the side wall of the courtroom. My footsteps echoed eerily on the hardwood floors, as I approached the bench.

The dais on which the judge sat, seemed unusually high and foreboding. His face was expressionless. He began to read the charges against me and all of the things that the State of New York could do to me, depending on my plea and the final judgment.

He read in a monotone voice that matched his expressionless face. I couldn't believe all the possible repercussions for a speeding ticket! As he droned on, the judgments of going to jail, etc., made me think maybe this wasn't such a good idea after all. I was starting to get that sinking feeling.

He finally finished his morose monologue. He looked down at me and said tonelessly, "How do you wish to plead?"

I looked him in the eyes. Then I looked away. I cleared my throat. Thoughtfully and honestly I said, "Well, before you said all that stuff, I was going to plead guilty. But now I'm not so sure!"

Once again, he began back at the beginning of his memorized horrors. When he got back to the "How do you wish to plead," part, I shrugged my shoulders, shook my head with resignation, and the sigh of being *caught red-handed*, and said, "Guilty."

I wanted so much to at least have something to say in my defense. But standing in front of the judge, I realized that I had absolutely nothing. I was guilty. No excuses. I could only throw myself on the mercy of the court.

As I entered my plea, I could swear I saw a slight smile wash across the judge's face.

"Your license, please," he continued.

"Oh no!" I thought. "He's going to 'mark' my license! This is gonna mean an increase in my insurance. It will also, for sure, mean more serious trouble if I ever get stopped again."

Quietly, the judge read and wrote. Then he looked down at me and said, "I'm adjusting your fine to $30.00. Please pay the clerk."

Humbly I said, "Thank you," and walked to the clerk's window.

The judge began to leave the dais and retire to his quarters, when the zealous clerk started waiving my license and calling out, "Oh Judge...Judge... You forgot to 'mark' her license!"

I could tell that she wasn't happy with the judge's fine reduction, and she wasn't about to stand for the license not being "marked."

The judge took the license and marked it appropriately.

❧

God, the Supreme Magistrate, often reduces my sentence, too. He makes the difficulty and payment severe enough that it's remembered, and hopefully not repeated. The lessons are imprinted. But the results are not so severe that they crush, or are unbearable.

It's often the on-lookers, who take things into their own hands and want to be sure that sufficient payment is inflicted. "Surely the judge has forgotten to 'mark' the license!"

❧

Lord, please help me see that only
You are my Judge. And You are merciful and good.
You are the Great and Mighty Judge upon the
throne who fixed the ticket that would have required
the death penalty for me.
When I stand before You, time and again with
offenses, in Your mercy, You adjust the fines to only
accomplish their necessary purposes.

I learn.

I grow.

You correct.

You forgive.

You restore.

I begin again.

When tongues wag and fingers point,
may I still look only to You
for my approval and my correction.
And Lord, please give me Your eyes and Your heart,
that I may never be a "tongue-wagger,"
or a "finger-pointer". And may I never question
Your ability or wisdom in disciplining
and caring for Your own.
Amen.

CHAPTER FIFTEEN

THE NAME CHANGE

"Is that your real name?"

My son, Doc, gets that a lot. Often people ask me too, "Why did you name your son, Doc?"

Being the smart mouth that I am, I answer, "Well, considering the other options, Dopey, Grumpy, Sleepy, etc. … I decided to go with Doc."

Actually, his given name is Brad. But in fourth grade, he claimed his new name, "Doc". We'd recently moved to Charlotte, North Carolina, and on the first day at his new school, when the teacher asked him his name, he told her, "My name is Doc." It stuck.

At first, when he told me he wanted to be called Doc, I humored it as a normal childhood whim, like "I want to be called Duke, Mom," a request that only lasts for a week or two, and then it's, "Call me B.C., Mom." Whatever. But this request was genuine and permanent. When his friends called, it was always for Doc. From that point on it was Doc, and it still is.

When I realized the change was here to stay, I asked him "Why did you change your name to Doc?"

He told me, somewhat surprised that I hadn't figured it out, "It's from Granddad."

"Oh!" I said. And the lights came on.

When my dad was a professor, many of his students affectionately called him Doc, instead of Dr. Sanders. Brad loved his Granddad. So besides the name just sounding "cool," the deeper reason was the family connection. As a little kid, he didn't realize he'd just given himself a PhD in the process.

ॐ

Have you ever thought about the way the Lord changed peoples' names in the scripture to fit a new stage or purpose in their lives?

Actually, He offers all of us a new family name... *Christ*ian. Taking on the name of our brother Christ, meaning "the anointed one," is a remarkable honor that comes from agreeing to be grafted into His family. If we accept the offer, we get the name.

There's a story told of Alexander the Great. On a certain occasion, a *defector* was captured and brought before him. He questioned the man.

"What is your name, soldier?" He demanded.

"Alexander, Sir" the soldier answered.

Alexander the Great rose to his feet and more fiercely shouted, "What is your name?"

"Alexander, Sir" came the sheepish reply.

"Enraged, Alexander the Great roared at the soldier, "What is your name?"

The soldier, in a whisper choked out, "Alexander, Sir."

Alexander the Great looked piercingly into the man's eyes, and said with power that cut the air, "Soldier! You Change Your Actions - Or You Change Your Name!"

❧

Oh Lord... Do my attitudes and my actions, my heart and my life, honor the family name?

Do I have the family traits? Do others look at me and say "anointed one - gift of love?"

౼

Father, Thank You for claiming me as Your own;
for stamping me with Your imprimatur;
for adopting me into Your family.
Thank You for Your wonderful patience with me.
It's truly my desire to honor the family name.
Forgive me when I fall short.
Thank You for being un-threaten-able
and unshakable.
Thank You for standing in the gap for Your children
and not disowning us when we don't measure up.
And thank You for loving me enough to teach me
Your ways so the family resemblance
can begin to show.
Who can dare accuse the King or the King's kids?
...For You cover our imperfections with Your
blanket of love... And Your Name Needs No
Defense. Amen.

CHAPTER SIXTEEN

THE RUBIK'S CUBE

"Well, Mom," he said. "I think it's sort of like a Rubik's Cube."

"A Rubik's cube?" I questioned.

Wait. ... Let me back up.

For most of my son's growing-up years, it was just the two of us. Often, I was being a kid, playing ball and doing kid stuff with him, and he was being a little adult, taking responsibility for me, beyond his years.

I tried not to lay heavy burdens on his willing young shoulders, but I didn't hide things from him either. I wanted him to experience life, strengths or struggles, from an honest, practical, perspective, and with a genuine understanding of God. We prayed together regularly about personal issues. One night, as we were getting ready to pray, I expressed some frustrations. I was feeling sorry for myself.

"I know we're supposed to rejoice in everything, but I'm not feeling very thankful tonight," I sighed.

My eleven-year-old was aware of crisis points, as we encountered this adventure called *life*.

Within a few weeks of having initiated what looked like a sure plan, each of the pivotal points had fallen like dominoes. I was back to square one.

In somewhat of a role reversal, my son responded, "Well mom, I think it's sort of like a Rubik's Cube."

"A Rubik's Cube?" I questioned.

"Yeah, a Rubik's Cube," he said, again. "See Mom, you can have your Rubik's Cube to where it looks like you only have a few moves to get everything into place. But when you start to make the moves, pretty soon your whole Rubik's Cube is all messed up again."

"But, if you gave your Rubik's Cube to the guy who made the Rubik's Cube, he would know what looks like only a few moves to you, is really about twenty-two...

And he knows which twenty-two!"

Wow! What can I say? What a gift my son is. And what a gift my God is.

୨

Forgive me for complaining, Lord.
My life does seem like a messed up Rubik's Cube
sometimes. I'm giving it back to You right now.
Thank You for putting my pieces into place...
Designer and Master of it all.
Forgive my lack of trust and my ungrateful heart,
when a few things don't go my way.
Your ways are not my ways,
but they're always working for my good.
You made me. You love me. You know me.
You plan for me. I'm truly in Your hands.
Thank You for making all the right moves,
putting all the colors in the right place,
in the right order,

Mighty,

Omnipotent,

Omniscient,

Lord of All.

Amen.

CHAPTER SEVENTEEN

THE CAMPING ESCAPADE

"Well, if you don't already have the equipment, don't buy any. We've have it all, and you're welcome to it," came the generous offer from my great neighbors.

The truth was I didn't have *any* camping equipment! I took them up on it.

I was anxious for my handsome, sandy-haired, ten-year-old son to experience Cape Hatteras National Seashore Campground with me. When I was a kid, it was a family tradition, our favorite vacation spot.

About a week later, when I was loading the tent into the car, I realized there wasn't any framework with it.

"Hmmm... That doesn't seem right. I've seen some clever pole systems before, but *no* pole system? I better go check this out," I thought.

I ran next door, hoping there was a simple solution.

"Yeah, *it does* have poles," my neighbors assured me, as we scoured their house looking for them. Finally, they concluded the poles must have been in their van - when it got totaled!

It was already after nine p.m. "What stores will be open?" I thought, somewhat frantically.

I hopped in the car and drove to the nearest place I could think of. It was a Zayre Discount Department Store...the Walmart of its day. I dashed into the store and raced up and down the aisles. No tents were on display. But I spotted some in boxes just as the announcement came, "Thank you for shopping at Zayre. Our store is now closing. Please bring your final purchases to the check-out counter at this time."

I scanned the pictures glued on the front of each box, and quickly chose one that looked perfect. It had two rooms. One was a big screened-porch and the other was sleeping quarters. I hoisted it from the shelf and made it out of the store...the last customer of the day.

"There. We made it!" I said to my son, as I closed the trunk. With the last camping treasures finally aboard, I smiled, "We're ready to leave for Hatteras in the morning!"

We left Charlotte excited to be on a once-in-a-life-time bonding adventure. We were creating memories! We only had to drive across the state of North Carolina, go over the huge bridge that links the mainland to the islands, and drive most of the way down the outer banks. Then the fun would begin! Somehow the trip took much longer than I remembered. And the drive to the outer banks stretched into dusk.

When I was a kid, the only way to get to the outer banks was by a ferry-boat. But now there's an extremely long bridge that connects the islands with the mainland. As we crossed, the wind lashed with incredible power.

"Gee, I can barely see anything. I hope there aren't any surprises. I'll try not to drive off the bridge," I mused to my son. But our spirits were undaunted and our hopes were high. We looked on the bright side and agreed, "Well, at least if it stops raining, this wind will dry out the sand!"

Sure enough, on the drive from the bridge to the campground, the deluge stopped, and the wind didn't. We cruised around the campground looking for just the right spot. "Oh look, Doc. There's a great site right at the edge of the sand dunes, facing the ocean!" We pulled in and claimed it.

By now, all remnants of sunlight were fading fast. "If we hurry, maybe we can get set up before it's completely dark," I thought out loud.

The sand was damp, but drying quickly in the forty-mile-an-hour winds. We began to unload. I pulled the tent out of the box, and as I did, a whole pile of poles came with it.

"Okay, let's see. First thing to do is to connect the poles and set the frame," I announced.

Normally, not much of a direction reader, I glanced through the poles to see if the assembly was obvious, and quickly surmised that *it was not*. I was going to have to resort to reading the directions! I pulled them out of the box and immediately two other problems surfaced. One was that other than some very sketchy diagrams, the instructions seemed to be in fluent Chinese, but very un-fluent English. So I studied the diagrams.

"Let's see. Insert pole A to pole B and pole C to pole A and pole D to pole B...Hmm..."

There wasn't that much difference between poles A, B, C, and D; very minor, although significant, I was sure. Finding the small differences, and assembling them correctly in tropical storm winds, was a challenge. And if I didn't hurry, I would get to do it at night, by flashlight too! The sun was going down fast!

It took both hands just to hold the directions. And if the instructions blew away, we were in real trouble.

"Hmm… I think it's going to take a few minutes to figure out how these poles fit together," I mumbled to myself. I decided to pull the tent over to the place we wanted to stake it.

"Let's be sure the screen room is facing the right direction," I yelled to Doc, through the wind, as we lifted up the front of the tent. "Whoosh!" Immediately the whole tent inflated like a huge balloon. We were holding on for dear life! Sure enough, the screen room was facing the right direction. That was the good news.

 But as I studied the flying beach house that momentarily threatened to launch us into a new version of Para-sailing, I noticed a pair of wings flapping on either side of it.

"What on earth are those?" I thought. Then I realized, the flaps blowing in the wind were the curtains that were supposed to separate the screen room from the sleeping room. And they were supposed to be on the inside, not the outside! That was the bad news.

"Doc," I announced, as calmly as I could, "They've packed this tent inside-out! How in the world are we going to turn it right-side-out in this wind?"

He responded back, as calmly as he could (we both were yelling at the top of our lungs to be heard over the wind). "No problem, Mom. I'll walk inside it and grab one of those window flaps. When I come back toward the door, just pull the tent over me in the opposite direction."

"Okay…Sounds like a plan!" I called.

So we began to initiate our craftiness. Doc walked inside and pulled the window flap back through the tent. As he did, of course, it changed the wind currents. What had been a fully inflated building - like walking in an air dome, suddenly collapsed! With the currents madly converging, I watched the flailing tent, beat, tangle, and engulf my son. Of course by this time, the whole campground thought we were crazy. We looked like an episode of Laurel and Hardy, The Three Stooges, and I Love Lucy, all rolled into one.

Later we discovered that we had, in fact, been the source of great entertainment, while we performed our unrehearsed, comedy routine.

But at last, someone came to our rescue!

"Could you use some help?" the rhetorical question came from a neighbor.

"Oh, thanks so much," I humbly accepted.

With a good Coleman lantern and a few extra hands, we were able to finish the job and settle in for a great vacation …one we never forgot!

We were so grateful for the couple who came to our rescue, in spite of what must have looked like something in between a bad sitcom, and insanity. (Not to speak of the work and the bad weather.)

They played the role of angels sent to help and protect us, when our circumstances were out of control. We were way out of our comfort zone on the, we-can-handle-this, scale.

What a God-send!

∾

When we needed equipment, God, You supplied.
But Lord, You knew in my heart,
I wanted my own tent. And when the poles were
missing, You supplied a new tent,
just in the nick of time.

As always, Your timing was perfect;
the problem solved, the supply given.
Then when the rain and wind made it almost
impossible, You stopped the rain.
But You let the wind blow hard, so the sand would
dry. And setting up the tent,
when we were beyond ourselves, again,
You sent some camping angels.
Surely, Your eye is on the sparrow, and I know
You're watching us.
Amazing, Wonderful, Lord.
Amen.

CHAPTER EIGHTEEN

THE MUFFLER

"Hello, Jan? I'm afraid we have some bad news. Granddad Fielden has passed away."

I was in the middle of a concert tour when the call came. The funeral was to be in two days in Philadelphia. My first thought was to jump in the car and go. But the facts, *reality*, gave me pause.

Living by faith, on "love offerings" from church to church, had been an exciting experience of seeing God's supply.

It seemed however, there was only ever enough to meet the basic needs – to get to the next church. No more. No less. It was daily bread, one slice at a time…Not the whole loaf.

At this particular time, (1984), my transportation was a 1969 Cadillac Eldorado that was loaded, (as in every inch was filled), plus a top-rack on the roof. It was moving-van, home, and transportation, as I sang my way from New York to California, the destination home base.

The car was a gift from a couple I hardly knew. It was a wonderful answer to prayer. But at this particular time, the dual muffler system had gone bad. It was loud. It was embarrassing. (Like, mothers would rush their children off the streets when they heard it coming.)

Anyway, having about $200 to my name, and the car in bad shape, I had some reservations about going. I knew it needed to be fixed, but this was a big exhaust system that would cost hundreds. I couldn't afford the repairs, and I hated driving it like it was.

Just gasoline and food for the trip would put a major dent in my net worth. ...But in the end, of course, I went.

Parking in Philadelphia is traditionally sparse, and this was no exception. I finally found a space down the street, a little way behind the funeral home.

Actually, I didn't want the family seeing or hearing the car, so it was okay with me to have it out of the mainstream. This was one time I didn't mind the walk.

However, showing up unannounced, I discovered the interment was going to be a half hour away, and all of the family cars driving to the cemetery, had been prearranged with the funeral home. They were full.

We were talking about it, when the funeral director overheard the conversation, and immediately offered to retrieve my car and bring it around to the processional line. What could I say? I explained where it was and gave him the keys.

In the middle of the service, I heard the noise...sort of like a space shuttle launch... and I knew it was my car! Fortunately, no one else did -Yet!

The service continued and despite my embarrassment, I was glad I had come. We filed out of the funeral home and cars began lining up to go to the cemetery. To conserve space, all of the vehicles had been backed up to the edge of the sidewalk. I started the engine to take my place in line. As the Eldorado moved forward, it rumbled louder than ever! Plus a horrible scraping sound had been added to the roar.

I got out and looked under the car and couldn't believe my eyes. Evidently, when the overloaded car had been backed up to the curb, the tailpipe hooked on it, buckled the entire exhaust system, and jammed the tailpipe up into the muffler. The scraping sound was the other end of the tailpipe etching it's signature into the pavement.

Before, the car was just loud and embarrassing. Now it was un-drivable! And, of course, with the expense of the trip, I for sure, didn't have enough money to fix it.

Tears ran down my face. I sat there crying. Then a song came to mind. I began singing softly...

"There's never a reason strong enough,

To ever stop praising the Lord.

Whenever the going's gettin' tough,

You gotta keep praisin' the Lord.

So praise Him.

You know that you should

Everything's workin' together for good.

So praise Him. You just gotta believe...

And never stop praisin' the Lord.

I sang it over and over, until the tears began to dry up.

About this time the funeral director walked across the street and got into his limo. I knew I had to tell him what happened and that my car was un-drivable.

"Come and get into the limousine," he said. "We'll have your car looked at while we're gone."

I didn't know how to tell him, I didn't have enough money to pay for any of this. As far as I was concerned, they could wire it back up with coat hangers and duct tape. But this was my grandfather's funeral. First things, first.

Most gratefully, I got into the lead limousine for the half hour drive to the cemetery, doors being opened and royal treatment all the way. I saw heads turn as I was chauffeured to the head of the line and knew the family must be thinking, "How'd she do that?"

After the final good-bye to Granddad, the limo delivered me to the muffler shop. I thanked the funeral director for his help and walked into the waiting room, dreading the news I was about to get from the clerk at the window.

"The gray Eldorado is mine," I informed her. "Do you have an estimate?" I continued.

She shoved the papers in front of me. I looked down and saw a total of $369.00, nearly twice what I had to my name.

Then I saw it. There was a *paid in full* stamped on the invoice, and the job was already done.

…All courtesy of the funeral home...

…And my God.

ॐ

Thank You, Lord.
Your sufficiency and Your provision out of the most incredible circumstances is amazing.
I'm awed.
Jehovah Jireh - God, my provider!
Thanks again…
Amen.

CHAPTER NINETEEN

THE CLERK

We approached the store while my mother recited the horrors of her last visit to the dress department.

"This woman is incredible! She doesn't want to help anybody. She's just as nasty as she can be. No matter when you approach her, if you ask for help, she has some reason she can't, or won't. She's always grumpy, and says, 'You'll just have to look for yourself.'"

Through the years, Mom's arthritis pain levels tend to make her a little on edge. Often, when she tries to shop, she'll just give up and leave the store. It's too hard. ...Too much pain ...Too hard to read the tags ...Too tiring.

On her last visit to this store though, as her energy was waning and her pain was increasing, she found a few items she really wanted to try on. But the dressing rooms were locked and the clerk was nowhere in sight.

Mom traipsed half way across the store before she spotted her. When she requested the clerk open the dressing rooms, the lady snapped, "I'll be there when I can." (Which was about half an hour - Okay, maybe it just seemed like that.)

"Anyway," Mom continued, "She acts like she's doing you a favor just to unlock the doors. I mean, isn't that the point? Isn't that part of her job? What does she think they're paying her for?"

There were obviously bad feelings on both parts. And now, during one of my visits home, we were entering the war zone again. The sales were so good we just couldn't resist. And history was about to repeat itself.

As usual, the fitting rooms were locked. This time I told Mom to wait. I would go and look for the lady in charge. And true to form, I found her half way across the store in a different department. However, I was sure if I engaged all my charm, I could evoke a better response.

Wrong!

She gave me the same response she gave Mom. By

the time I returned, a long line of people were waiting in front of the dressing rooms. Mom later relayed the ugly, impatient comments that had flowed.

When the lady arrived, though, everyone put on their happy faces, and the dressing room frenzy began. Mom and I were first in line. Strangely enough, the clerk passed out garment tickets and opened rooms for everyone, *but us*.

Mom was steamed! She was still angry from the last time, before we even started on today's match. Her nasty spirit was a sure rival for the clerk's.

Mom's derogatory comments continued. She talked to me, not the lady directly, and but loudly enough for the clerk and everyone else to hear.

So, I tried "the look," on Mom. That didn't work. Then, I tried the "It's okay. Don't worry about it," approach. That didn't work, either. The comments kept flowing. Finally, when the rest of the line was accommodated, we were allowed to enter the prized dressing rooms. We escaped the battle with only minor casualties and some great bargains.

On the way home, I said to Mom, "You know, there's got to be a reason why that lady is the way she is. I wonder what it is? I wonder what's happened in her life - or what she's going through right now? She seems so angry and sad. Basically, she does a good job, if it wasn't for her attitude."

My mother is very outspoken and blunt. She doesn't have a mean heart, but she gets impatient. Anyway, that was the end of the discussion.

A week or two later, it was still working on her, though. Yes, what did she know of this woman's life? Maybe she had suffered, or *was* suffering great things. What kind of sad life might she have? Maybe she's never gotten encouragement or compliments from anyone.

Mom returned to the store. This time she was on a mission! She found the clerk.

"I'm sure you remember me. A little while ago I was in here and I was very impatient and unkind. My attitude with you was not nice at all."

The lady responded, "Oh, I don't even remember."

Mom said, "Well, I remember. And I want you to forgive me for how nasty I was."

She explained how hard it was for her to shop. Then they began to talk and share things about their lives.

She was responsible for multiple departments, which explained the locked dressing rooms and her being in other parts of the store. She also shared that she'd recently lost her mother to cancer. With more information on the table, Mom was able to sincerely say, "You do a great job. This department is always well organized and displayed. The store must be very happy with the job you do for them."

"I wonder if she's ever heard a word of praise in her life?" Mom later commented to me.

Before the conversation in the store ended that day, she repeated again how sorry she was that she had been such a *pain*.

Mom could see the Lord was at work. She was aware that *the love she felt was from Him*. It was so healing, so joyful, so special.

"I want to do something for her. I just don't know what it is yet," Mom continued. "If that little lady knew how much I've cried over this, she wouldn't believe it."

In relating the story to me, tears ran down her face while she relived the feelings.

How wonderful to experience such a change in two hearts. How great it is when Mom goes to that store now, she mostly looks forward to seeing the clerk. Finding bargains has been de-throned.

꒰

Thank You, Lord.

You still give sight to our blind eyes.

You still melt our cold hearts.

You still redeem our days with Your love.

Amen.

CHAPTER TWENTY

THE GIRL IN SHEEP'S CLOTHING

Fall had arrived in upstate New York. The air was crisp and the leaves were magnificent. The sky was clear and bright. It was a Sunday afternoon and my twelve-year-old son, Doc, and I, headed on an adventure-ride toward Cooperstown, New York. I threw the camera in the car and hoped to catch some of the fantastic colors as we drove.

When we arrived in Cooperstown, we made a left that carried us up into the beautiful hills that surround the quaint Baseball Hall of Fame hamlet. I had a good friend from high school who lived out that way and decided to stop for a surprise visit.

Yeah ...Surprise! No one was home.

But as I took in the beauty of the setting, I noticed that just behind the house, rolling hills bolstered huge rocks, and gorgeous trees flashed with crimson, yellows and oranges. Grazing in the middle of the field, was a herd of sheep and a couple of cows.

"Hey, I've got an idea, Doc," I called, as I climbed out of the car and grabbed the camera. "I think this might be just the place to get a picture for my new album cover."

I was trying to decide on a title and cover shot. "Gift of Love" or "Shepherd of Love" were the two ideas that topped the list.

"If I decide on "Shepherd of Love," a cover picture of me in my sheepskin vest, nestled among real sheep would work great, huh?" I said with enthusiasm.

I had on a cream colored turtleneck with my sheepskin vest, a pair of jeans, and high-healed espadrilles that were open-toed and opened-heeled.

And there it was right in front of us… sheep, hills, rocks, and beautiful fall colors. I was dressed for the occasion, as if it had been planned.

Doc didn't say much of anything, but seemed okay with it and went along. We climbed the fence and were ready for the challenge.

I carefully managed the rough terrain in my impractical shoes.

The sheep eyed us with great suspicion when we began to get close. There was one ram that stood guard over the rest of the sheep. The sheep gathered together behind him as we approached. I talked to them, trying to calm them, and explained that we only wanted a photo.

"It's okay, little babies. We just want to take your picture. We're not going to hurt you. You're so beautiful," I went on in my gentlest tones. "I'd love to have you in my picture. You'll be the stars!" I reassured them and kept telling them how beautiful they were, while I inched nearer. (By now, you probably think I talk to plants and hug trees too, right?)

The look of suspicion and mistrust from the ram was unmistakable. It shouted a warning to the flock-

BAA! BAA!! INVASION! DANGER! DANGER!!

No amount of reassuring could stop the race from one end of the field to the other. Every time I got close enough to think Doc might be able to get a shot, the ram took off running and baaing, and the sheep followed.

We tracked that herd all over the field, in the most unobtrusive way we knew how. Finally, I sat down in the middle of them, and Doc snapped a couple of shots.

"Mission accomplished! We did it!"

We were congratulating ourselves when Doc glanced to his left. With a somewhat shocked look, he shouted, "Mom! That's not a cow! It's a bull! And he's after you!"

Doc bolted for the fence, which was about 20 yards away. There were several reasons I didn't bolt, however. He was twelve. I was thirty-four. He was standing. I was sitting. He was wearing Nikes. I was wearing high-heeled espadrilles. And for whatever reason, thankfully, the bull seemed only focused on me, not him.

I looked to my right. My eyes met those of a very angry animal. He was still small by bull standards, but a lot bigger than me! He stood staring at me, head down, snorting and scraping his front hooves in the dirt, preparing for the charge. I felt like I should at least have a red cape!

He was considerably closer to me than I was to the fence. His intentions were clear. I slowly got to my feet. Bolting for the fence like Doc did, would mean turning my back on the bull, which didn't strike me as a very good idea! I also couldn't imagine trying to *run* over that rough terrain in those crazy shoes, while at the same time knowing full well, that even under the best of circumstances, *I couldn't out-run a bull!*

Maybe the best plan was to back slowly toward the fence, keep my eye on the bull, and try not to stumble backwards. My mind raced and my heart pounded. Fear reared its ugly head. I sat there with various options running through my brain. But as I tried to figure out the best approach, something different happened. I distinctly felt that it was time to take command, not time to run.

A new thought was definitely being impressed on me. "Hasn't God given us dominion over all land and animals? And isn't obedience, in the name of Jesus, the Creator of everything, recognized by *His* animals?"

I looked the bull in the eyes and said in an un-intimidated voice, "In the name of Jesus, you stop!"

The bull looked startled. Then once again, he began with the head down, snorting, hoof-scraping business, and took a few steps forward, as if to call my bluff. I took a few steps backwards, but then stopped and firmly said again, "In the name of Jesus Christ, you stop."

I almost surprised myself, as I felt the calm authority of my words. The bull looked puzzled.

A third time, I spoke the words with confidence. "In the name of Jesus Christ, you stop!"

The bull stood perfectly still and seemed suddenly calm. I kept my eye on him, walked slowly towards the fence, and climbed over.

Hugs! Great relief!

❧

The thought that struck me immediately after my escape, was how accurate the Lord is when he likens us to sheep.

At first I was amazed and amused with the crafty, in-control, cagey, suspicious ram, and how he passed his attitude on to the sheep.

How often are we tempted to follow a "ram"? How often do we succumb to someone we consider to be an authority? How often do we get in step with someone who encourages us to mentally, physically, emotionally, and/or spiritually follow them? And then, when we come to our senses, we realize that the "ram," is only leading a ridiculous exercise in arrogance, manipulation and control.

We're taught to live life being wary, only we call it being *wise*. In truth, our wisdom may only be a disguise for fear. The Lord, our Gentle Shepherd says, "Fear not, for I am with you always."

I've been at both extremes of fear. I've been afraid of the benign, but also walked *where angels fear to tread.*

Why is it so easy for me to listen to a "ram" and pay no attention to the Good Shepherd? The girl in sheep's clothing walked into true danger and was sitting in the middle of it taking pictures. -Didn't consult the Shepherd on that one! It never even crossed my mind.

Yes, I admit it! I'm like the sheep! I think I'm so clever, so perceptive, so competent, so in control. And the fact is, I'm not. I often walk right into the middle of trouble with no awareness of it. In fact, I often come to my senses only when the situation reaches a crisis.

I climbed over the fence and into the field, aware I knew nothing about the animals. I knew I didn't have on very good shoes. I was also aware I should probably find out who the animals belonged to, and get photo permission, as I was sure they didn't belong to my friend. But at the time, it seemed like too much red tape, too big a deal for just a few pictures. -Besides, what if they said "No"? (And likely they would have.) I'm sure they would have at least supervised, or mentioned, "Watch out for the bull!"

I can see the Lord's description of me is accurate. I am sheep-like. I need His rod, not a ram, to move me when there's true danger. I need His staff to rescue me when I get stuck, fall over the cliff, face peril, or "bull".

I need the Good Shepherd.

౨

Lord, I rejoice in Your knowledge of me.
Thank You for still loving me and caring for me in
spite of my stubborn, foolish, sheep-likeness.
I want to listen only to Your voice.
Please forgive my willful stupidity, Lord,
and the times I block You out, or listen to
other voices, and miss the truth.
...Gentle Shepherd, come and lead us.
For we need Your help to find our way. Amen.

Psalm 23

"The Lord is my shepherd; I shall not want.

He makes me to lie down in green pastures;

He leads me beside the still waters.

He restores my soul;

He leads me in the paths of righteousness

For His name's sake.

Yea, though I walk through the valley

of the shadow of death, I will fear no evil;

For You are with me;

Your rod and Your staff, they comfort me.

You prepare a table before me

in the presence of my enemies.

You anoint my head with oil;

My cup runs over.

Surely goodness and mercy shall follow me

All the days of my life;

And I will dwell in the house of the Lord Forever."

ABOUT THE AUTHOR

J. Brooke-Harte

Jan grew up as a P.K. (preacher's kid) and started performing in church at the age of four. She's enjoyed singing and speaking at churches across the country, including The Crystal Cathedral in Garden Grove, California, Angeles Temple in Los Angeles, and Fourth Presbyterian Church, in Bethesda, Maryland.

Variety and versatility describe her life. Jan's experiences range from singer/recording artist, actress, marketing/public relations director, and entrepreneur, to youth pastor, college Dean of Students, author, counselor, and founder of The Foundation Association, Inc.

Jan writes children's books, poetry and apologetics, as well as life stories. Her foremost desire is to direct peoples' eyes to her first love, Jesus Christ. Encouragement is her call.

"As the deer pants after the water brooks, So pants my soul for You, O God." Psalm 42:1

HAND IN THE COOKIE JAR

HAND IN THE COOKIE JAR

HAND IN THE COOKIE JAR

www.ingramcontent.com/pod-product-compliance
Lightning Source LLC
Chambersburg PA
CBHW031515040426
42445CB00009B/244